Beauty in 1

Special Thanks

To whomever is reading this right now, thank you so much. It means the world to me. This book wouldn't have been possible without all the love and support I have received over the years. I have compiled a short list of names and if yours isn't on here, it's because I'm saving it for book two: Jude Aquilina, Marie Baker, Josh Beauchamp, Alicia Bird, Sarah Brown, David Drake, Keenan Drake, Sheema Karasu, Steven Lengyel, Wanling Liu, Brenda Matthews, Stephen Matthews, Laura Moniuszko, Brian O'Neill, Tom Rees and Jill Wherry.

Acknowledgements

Some of the poems in this collection have previously been published. Thanks go to the following:
'Cards', 'Our Song', 'Those Fateful Words', 'To the Woman' and 'Twinkle Twinkle' were anthologised in
Tea Tree Gully Poetry Festival 2017: Selected Poems,
edited by Sharon Kernot, North Eastern Writers Inc.
'The Lie' was anthologised in *Wild*,
edited by Joan Fenney, Ginninderra Press, 2018.
'Mon Amour' and 'My Addiction' were anthologised in
Dream-Water Fragment: Friendly Street Poets 42
(edited by Ros Schulz & Karl H, Cameron-Jackson), 2018.
'40 Seconds' was featured in February 2018
on http://www.holdenhillmedia.com.au

Beauty in the Darkness
ISBN 978 1 76041 691 1
Copyright © text Andrew Drake 2019

First published 2019 by
GINNINDERRA PRESS
PO Box 3461 Port Adelaide 5015
www.ginninderrapress.com.au

Contents

Those Fateful Words

I could never write a new chapter,
no matter how long it took
as you were never just a footnote,
you were the whole goddam book.
So instead I will tear out the page
with those fateful words The End,
then fold the paper till you have wings
so I can watch you ascend.

I will rest my head on your novel
in the time I see you fly,
feeling the distant breeze carry you
until you become the sky.
However, you're never white or grey,
you're only out of the blue,
as there's nothing cloudy or vivid
in these images of you.

And so when the sky begins to dim
I will know you've travelled far,
deep into the dark infinity,
to become my shining star.
Then I'll hold your story one last time
before you and I depart,
so I can replace your final page
with my origami heart.

40 Seconds

Here's something you don't usually hear. Over a million people each year. 40 seconds is all it takes until another one has died from a suicide.

And three-quarters of them were men who were told to man up when it was hard enough to speak up.

And when he's crying, they just stare and tell him to grow a pair rather than letting him share the reasons why he's hurting so much… Making him believe that he should hide his feelings of suicide.

Saying boys don't cry is one of the reasons why they cry alone. It's one of the reasons why they die alone. Because they feel like they have nobody to phone as they're too busy being taught that sticks and stones are the only things that can break their bones. 40 seconds…another one just died.

She was taught that she hits like a girl, throws like a girl, drives like a woman and everything in between. And she knows that she doesn't look anything like those girls in that magazine. She was told to stay in the kitchen like a good wife, and when she killed herself they were shocked, believing she had the perfect life. They had said that she wasn't ladylike regardless of the facts that she is a lady no matter how she acts. And he, he is a man in my eyes, no matter how much he cries. But it wouldn't matter if they were a dude or a chick because they are more than just a statistic. Another 40 seconds. Another one just died.

They were strong for far too long and so when I hear people say that their swansong was wrong, I say all of their songs were beautiful. So for the ones we've lost, I'm so sorry. For the ones we could lose, I say that you don't need to live in fear because there are people for you here. And to everyone else, we don't just say R U OK for one day in a year. Silence is the silent killer. For words can hurt, but they can also save a life.

Fortress

Our love is like a fortress
it will stand the test of time.
But you and I aren't made of stone;
I'm the dozen to your dime.
I was just your quarter
while you were my whole
and now I am truly spent
at the cost of your soul.

It's funny how we're broken
and yet belong together
for no matter what I do
we will be trapped forever
in these evil walls
this fortress that we built –
there's no escape for you and I
this is where we wilt.

Many loves are in this world
but nothing compares to you
and yet I searched in vain
for another love that's true.
So here we stay, apart as one
we burn in parallel
our fortress walls contained our fire
and stood strong as we fell.

Mon Amour

Each individual's life is unique
and though born lineal, they hold mystique,
inherently following a motif
that time is consequential, although brief.

For, as this paradox is unravelled,
we learn from every story travelled,
constantly weaving intricate tangles,
intertwining our specific angles
and neglecting the final narrative,
as death does not have a comparative.

Because, the afterlife has no wordsmiths,
so posthumously lives are but heard myths,
based on montages that often reveal
how each memory spent had made them feel.

Immortalising us in mystery
and thus creating our own history
that was made through another's dominion,
because all we are is an opinion.
So after our time has come, mon amour
I wonder what we'll be remembered for…

Cards

I was 21 when I saw her sitting at the deck. Her beauty made my knees fold, as I became a wreck. I was in my best suit; she could see me in plain sight. I shuffled over to her so I could play my cards right. I was such a joker, with 52 pick-up lines. But she raised to walk away, to say that she declined. I thought it was a bust, but I called out just in case. Turns out that my gamble worked as she just liked the chase. She, in time, became my queen; we were two of a kind. So I went out and bought the biggest diamond you could find. I held her perfect hand, I didn't know where to start. I gently whispered to her 'my love, you have my heart'. To have and to hold was a risk that I was dealt. I bet my entire life on the love that I had felt. We became a full house and I became the king. Until she hit me with the news and handed back the ring. I tried to hold a poker face as she began to split. But I was just too flushed so I forced her to submit. My heart was out of luck, my diamond now repaid, as I reached for a club then finally a spade.

Dear Mum

Dear Mum,

Remember that time when I was one? When I learnt how to crawl, walk then run?

Nah, you were too busy smoking your joints and drinking your rum because having a son wasn't your kind of fun. That's why you decided to run.

I remember seeing you next when I was 6. It was Mother's Day and I had built you a house made out of popsicle sticks. But you were up to your old tricks, throwing it down to the ground like a ton of bricks because it didn't cost money. It's funny… because it taught me to appreciate handmade gifts.

I remember your mug when you offered me drugs instead of hugs. I was only 10 but by then I knew never to be like you. So I said no.

Where were you when I was hit by a car? Seeing stars, getting scars. It wasn't even bizarre any more for you to be so far, and I thank my lucky stars because you deserve everything that you are. It's a shame, I doubt you even know my son's name. It's as if this whole life was just a game to you and, through it all, I'll never be the same as you because I overcame your self-righteous blame and the shit you put me through.

So thank you, Mum, for teaching me how to never be.

Because I was there for my son when he started to walk, I listened to him talk and I watched him like a hawk. I was there every step of the way, every single day because there is no way I wouldn't stay to watch him grow, because I love him so.

And I'll still be there when he has a son and I'll take care of my grandson. I'll watch him crawl, walk then run. Because I know that I'll never become anything like you, Mum.

GPS

I am constantly travelling
with no destination in sight,
not a map to where I'm going
or knowledge to which way is right.
I end up walking in circles
that are never truly the same
because no matter where I head
I've remembered where I came.

But in the centre of each loop
is a world that I dream to view,
to navigate through this journey
so that I can be lost in you,
my home without a GPS
where I'm able to find my way
so that I can finally stop
in the place where I long to stay.

Follow You

Our worlds are parallel
I feel you next to me
in all my yesterdays
and every memory.

Bent but never broken
our circles stay aligned
linking in symmetry
becoming intertwined.

I'll always follow you
just as day follows night
walking through the darkness
as you walk through the light.

Diverging from this life
upon your suicide,
waiting for tomorrow
for our hearts to collide

while breathing in today
each moment that you gave,
until we meet again
through love beyond the grave.

Moonlit Shore

On this moonlit shore,
I felt the ocean's silence
but at least it waved.

Conditional Love

The Newlyweds

He would have done anything he could
to stop his dad from marrying her.
But his warnings were misunderstood,
turned against him by a usurper.
Through her psychological mind game,
an ultimatum had been devised,
with the son kicked out and love to blame;
the father was truly compromised.

Condition one: manipulation.
I won't love a mental abuser.
Words are never just a narration
when coming from that of a user.

The Lovers

My one, my only and other half,
with you I promise I'll always stay,
the lover had typed on her behalf
to her other third when she would stray.
These messages made her partner smile,
though he knew it meant she'd come home late.
I love you too, was his lover's style,
sent back so that he could fornicate.

Adultery is condition two,
I will not stand for lies and deceit.
Love is not something you misconstrue
and neither is an unfaithful cheat.

The Bible-basher

He loved his daughter and God above
which filled her heart with joy and fear.
She gave him unconditional love
while he beat her for being a queer.
He would preach that love was colourless
to a canvas he left black and blue,
and all that she had done was confess
a real love to one that was untrue.

Condition three is abusive hate.
I will not love a violent heart.
For no amount of pain can negate
who we are from birth till we depart.

The Epilogue

We were brought up in a precast land,
learning a concept so outdated –
that unconditional love is grand
and thus should never be debated.
But hearts don't live by another's rules,
they can never be forced to endure
these preconceived notions made by fools,
based upon fear by the insecure.

So I will not love a narcissist,
one so pompous, pretentious and vain
and not a degrading masochist
who thrives in humiliating pain.
Nor a hypocritical racist
who's bigoted, resentful and vile;
a complete dogmatic chauvinist
or a deplorable paedophile.

I hold no love for one so selfish,
greedy and materialistic
and neither will I love or relish
those who are callous and sadistic.
I will not stand for vulgarity
whether indecent or ignorant
and I am against brutality,
the malicious and belligerent.

For every second my heart beats
my love will be untraditional
and this I promise never depletes
because real love is conditional.
Therefore, I will love those who are brave,
the courageous and also the shy;
the ones who have been hurt, yet forgave
with the beauty on which we rely.

I'll love the sweet and benevolent
with generous, compassionate souls
as well as ones who are prevalent
in helping others achieve their goals.
I adore those with an open mind,
thoughtful, not just theoretical.
People who are genuinely kind,
trustworthy and sympathetical.

And I love the fact that love is pure,
as it is taught and so we have learnt
that real love will never have a cure
for it isn't just given, it's earnt.

Our Song

A myriad of people
will dance to a single song,
to which I have no rhythm
in a place I don't belong.

They all swayed to the music
while I tangled at the feet,
when suddenly you walked by
and my heart danced to your beat.

Through a melody of hope,
I saw a sweet admission
which sang serendipity
between your composition.

And so we flawlessly waltzed,
till no one was left in sight.
Your tune became our anthem
as we danced into the night.

To My Tomorrow

To my tomorrow, with your lonesome breeze
I beg of you to carry me please
let me feel cool wind blowing as I shift
away from this place, alone in your drift.

Where am I headed? I do not recall,
as long as you're here, anywhere at all
I'll look forward to when I can erase
the misery felt in my yesterdays.

But what of today? Why are you so calm?
I am a mess, surely that should alarm.
Yet everything's still, today will not end.
Gone with the wind, serenity's friend.

Beyond the Light

I wonder what is beyond the light,
from darkness with still pulse;
I imagine a destination
created by impulse

where we travel towards nirvana,
from our mortality
to reach a utopian vision,
our new reality.

Here multicolours are invented
to quash the black and white
so may you lift your feet off the ground
and take your rainbow flight.

I know that we will meet at the end,
my love, my other half.
In truth there will always be a smile
forever be a laugh.

And so I will plan our rendezvous,
while hearing final breath
though your heart may stop, mine beats for you
throughout life, on through death.

Perpetual Vacancy

We live in a world of perpetual vacancy
where we have become the shadows of complacency,
from silent victims that are too paralysed to speak,
to the forced who were taught self-expression makes them weak.
We were forbidden the day we became reliant
and are punished in each moment that we're defiant.

Eradicated from individuality
then given freedom without originality –
and while most of us have conformed, by definition,
we still hold onto a natural disposition
of society's standards and what is neglected
when peace is so simple and yet often rejected.

For selfish greed holds an imaginary power,
a perception turned conception that made us cower.
So let's break free as I am unable to pretend
refusing to quiet to enable and defend.
I will reveal the truths about others' perfections
how we've strived for theirs rather than our own reflections.

It's because we can see respect through a false ideal
yet lack the confidence to believe in what is real,
but I will not be told as no more am I scared
and I will fight until universal love is shared,
as you cannot force someone to love the way you do
but they can feel your emotions in all that is true.

So if we could not understand what has been displayed
with our opinions differing in all we've conveyed
then I will hold you, to my body and to your word,
as we don't need to agree, we just need to be heard.

Twinkle Twinkle

Twinkle twinkle little star, how I wonder what you are.

So I googled it, Wikipediaed it, I asked Jeeves, checked with bing, brought it up with Siri and put an ad about it on Craiglist but I didn't bother with Yahoo, and I found out that on this starry starry night, there is a fault in our stars.

I mean, just look at the stars, look how they shine for you, for when you wish upon a star, your dreams come true,

except for the fact that they're most likely already dead and even though video killed the radio star, it certainly didn't kill these ones.

I'm not saying there was some kind of Star Wars, they were just burnt out. Literally.

And I learnt that the most famous star is the sun. I mean here comes the sun, here comes the sun and it's all right because although I might get a blister in the sun, there ain't no sunshine when she's gone.

However, before she's gone, the sun will expand, becoming a red giant and destroying the whole planet!

But don't worry, the radiation and heat will kill us way before then. And anyway, that's millions of years away because, right now the sun is still young, it's just a child star and it helps us immensely.

So, to the sun, you are a superstar, that is what you are, and one day, I'll be your starman, waiting in the sky.

But right now, thanks to you, I'm walking on sunshine, and don't it feel good?

My Lonely Bedbug

She was my lonely bedbug,
crawling under empty sheets,
leaving memories behind
for everyone she meets,
as I slept on the floorboards
dreaming of her on my skin,
while I lived like a termite,
isolated in my sin.

My world was never like hers,
breaking homes was all I knew
till her home came crashing down,
crushing me without a clue.
She was close enough to love
but far enough to be blind,
for together we belonged
in a dream she'll never find.

The Puppet Master

Dance for me my puppet, follow as I lead
I will manipulate, your feet until they bleed.
Your simple-minded nature, is easy to control
while I have become master, you too will learn your role

You act because I pull your strings, I made you who you are.
You never achieved anything, yet now you are a star.
And all you do is stand there, getting praise for my work
while I choose to be hidden, high above my cirque.

You were just a tangled mess, lost in single thread
till I weaved this special rope, then tied it round your head;
your prison's in my fingers, your life now in my hands
you will never rest until you follow my commands.

You could free yourself, unshackle from your chain
but you will never choose this fate, you're born to entertain.
And so I will continue and you will never fret.
This is the only life you lead, you're just a marionette.

You chose indecision; you once had your chance,
now you have an audience, so dance puppet dance.

Waves

I felt you carry me,
like waves of the ocean,
when all this commotion
was drowning in the sea.

I watched you hold me tight
when the tide pulled me in.
Your water met my skin,
then vanished from my sight.

I heard you nevermore,
as silence lost its way.
I drifted far away
while you reached for the shore.

And I knew you were gone,
while sinking in the blue,
when all I loved to view
could not be looked upon.

Beauty of the Fallen

She started in the darkness and she ended in the night
the fallen angel finally can take her final flight.
The world has lost a beauty, as she was one of a kind,
and in a hundred thousand years, another you won't find.

With future all but over, I start clinging to her past
in a world full of contradictions, she is free at last.
And yet it's not as black and white when filled with shades of grey
as she's so missed that even the non-religious will pray.

Many times her single tears had shed from dusk until dawn,
but now it is the whole world that keeps weeping as they mourn.
I never would have realised forever hurts so much
until I learnt that there will never be a final touch.

It is not fair for me to smile with knowledge that she cried,
and it isn't fair for me to live knowing that she died.
For I know her time on this earth was tragically stolen,
but I will never forget the beauty of the fallen.

Superstitious Slave

You will always be my queen
and a superstitious slave.
You've been this way since thirteen
all the way into the grave.
You were found 'neath a ladder
with a mirror that shattered,
and this only gets sadder
because your black cat scattered.

I had never understood
until this all came in threes,
so I'm knocking on the wood
of your coffin on my knees.
I don't believe in magic
or a placebo effect,
but when all things are tragic
it is time to resurrect.

So I will break every rule,
I will step on every crack,
I will face all that is cruel
so that I can have you back.
I will fix your looking glass
with all of my affection,
for our time will never pass
till I see our reflection.

Happiness and Sorrow

We all have a choice between happiness and sorrow,
what I chose yesterday I will not choose tomorrow.
For today is the day where I search for what is true,
with lies, the faded memories that I won't pursue.

I've decided to discover the good this world holds,
coming out of the shadows to witness what unfolds,
and as I overcome all the hurdles that I climb,
I'll remember to keep smiling, one day at a time.

My Hero

for my son

How am I able to explain
the war that has consumed my brain
to the one who has touched my heart?

That every single smile you gave
is all of the love that I crave,
yet sometimes I still fall apart.

Because mothers and fathers cry,
we make mistakes yet always try
but some things we can't overcome.

And though you can't stop every tear,
it means the world to have you here,
as Dad loves you and so does Mum.

I wonder when you hold my hand
if it's because you understand
and therefore go to any length

to make sure that I know you're there
by holding me to show you care,
as each touch of yours gives me strength.

And one day it will be your turn
to realise the truth and learn
that the real hero wasn't me.

As you're the one I look up to,
the one I admire through and through
and the one I aspire to be.

When the Rain Comes

He believed he was a blank canvas, the world was his paintbrush and each story splattered against him like paintballs. These multicoloured bullets came raining down, leaving him black and blue with a hint of hue, and a rainbow across his heart.

He tried scrubbing the pain away, the paint away, wishing the rainbow would stay, but it wouldn't wash off, it wouldn't wash off, it wouldn't wash off, it won't wash off.

He scrubbed so hard that the colours were replaced with calluses and he, the canvas evolved into a clean slate. But slates don't flutter in the wind the way canvases do and so when these stories TOOK AIM and FIRED, every multicoloured bullet that rained down would wash off, it would wash off, it would wash off, it washed off. The black, the blue, the rainbow too, because slates are heavier than any colour in the world.

So instead he decided to carve his name into the slate so it would never wash off before burying his stories, six foot deep. His slate became his gravestone because he buried his feelings until his loved ones had to bury him.

However, these stories aren't only his, they're ours too.

But you are not a story to read through.

You are not a canvas to paint on.

You are not a slate to carve in.

You are not a gravestone to lay under

and you are not the artist,

you are the art.

So when the rain comes, be what will never wash off.

Because you do not paint rainbows,

no,

you are the rainbow.

34

If I Could

If I could listen to your heartbeat
    and then tell you that I understand,
would you believe me or would you leave me
    until I placed my heart in your hand?

If I held you every second
    and showed you that I will not let go,
would you push me aside or would you hide
    until you embraced your sorrowful woe?

If I kissed you in each place that aches
    and let you see yourself through my eyes,
would you open yours or would you pause
    until I proved that mine held no lies?

If I could take all the pain away
    and love you beyond your depression,
would all of your fear slowly disappear
    until you begin your progression?

If you watched me as I fall apart
    and then ask me how I can still smile,
would you want to know each piece I let go
    was to build you until you felt worthwhile?

And if you're unable to believe
    and you feel that love won't go this far,
I will be the one who will never run
    until you learn how beautiful you are.

Elixir

In you I had my home sweet home
till the darkness caught my fire.
The lights went out as I switched off,
igniting truth in the liar.

Your poison was the elixir
while my flame created flashes.
I watched my cure burn to the ground
before scattering the ashes.

A Thousand Cuts

I was created, then invaded
humiliated and degraded
I was shown the dark, but found the light
I was given blade but would not fight
I was cut so deep, I never waned
when I stood my ground, red fountains rained.

What I held onto, what I let go
what I believed in welcomed sorrow;
I was taught to hate, I learnt to love
I was fed to wolves yet sent a dove.
They still continue, they never cease
they want the one thing I won't release.

Integrity left, with stars in eyes
I'm tortured for it with scars and lies.
It's such a rare gift, they speak, they hiss
their devilish plot, their new found bliss.
Relinquish your soul, let go, begin,
your freedom awaits when you give in.

Yet still I refuse, I have spoken…
My mind may be lost, my heart broken
but I'll die this way. One thousand scars,
a beautiful end, to join the stars.
I will match the wounds they gave to me
with a thousand cuts, my guarantee.

Then watch as my eyes finally welt
releasing the pain I've always felt.
The freedom I see, the love I feel
that runs down my cheeks, that makes it real.
So with final cut, I chose my path
escaping this world, free from their wrath.

There are many things they cannot learn
as ideals like mine you only earn,
they can't be taken, for you must give.
So I give my soul so it can live.
Perfect in my death through bloodied knife…
a pure end to my imperfect life.

Shadow in the Night

I welcomed you to the sun, hoping you would roam
making wild assumptions that this must be your home.

Your perfection follows me in a silhouette
it's all I've ever wanted, everything and yet
something isn't right, something unintentional
for when I look at you, you're two dimensional.

You cannot be real though I have no objections
as there's nothing more perfect than imperfections.
They're what make you special and yet you stay behind
ensuring that all of our footsteps have aligned.

I often wonder when you disappear from sight,
are you solely being my shadow in the night?
Or are you everything that I could never see
as it's in the darkness that you're finally free.

Food for Thought

Live as if it's your first meal and never fear your last.
Any meal that left bad taste should be left in the past.
It may be used as food for thought but never at the helm
as this poisoned spice of life can completely overwhelm.

You may think there is one recipe to life used as law
but the way to happiness is found in a thousand more.
You need to taste all there is to offer on your plate
And when it is in front of you, do not hesitate.

You'll find that each cuisine will have its own distinct flavour.
Welcome the new and hold onto ones you want to savour.
We are dished up much and forget we're given a knife
to use in cutting right through the banquet that is life.

Sometimes we're full and other times we feel we have the least.
Either way you should never let it stop you from the feast.
So relish every meal and know that in each breath
second guessing hunger for life is to starve to death.

Muffle You Out

These beige paper-thin walls cannot muffle you out.

The TV is on full blast, showing reruns of clichéd TV shows about happy families and happy days and they still cannot muffle you out.

The old ceiling fan is spinning so fast that it's shaking without rhythm, but the loud winds that blow cannot muffle you out.

The paper that blows across the room, colliding with the beige paper-thin walls and the TV cannot muffle you out.

The note I wrote on one of those pieces of paper, for you, that is held down by the headphones that could never quite drown out your voice

and your screams, bounce from the vibrations of the TV and sway in the breeze, but this not cannot muffle you out.

The grip on the handle of your revolver, the single bullet in your chamber, the finger on your trigger and the absence of your muffler cannot muffle you out.

But the bullet that travels through me, through the TV, through the switch of my ceiling fan and escapes through the now red paper-thin walls, finally silences you.

The Actors

Her facade was to act the part,
with her heart never a factor.
Because her world was fictional
as she played that of an actor.
For our script was based on the truth,
'twas a love story with a twist
as the love was never written
until our hearts couldn't resist.
Yet for that very brief moment,
I could see she wasn't acting
when she looked deep into my eyes
and found them to be distracting.
But she couldn't break character,
developing a broken heart
as the story that was written
had us gradually depart.
However, in that final scene
when we weren't actors any more,
I searched those eyes for what was real
then pulled her in for an encore.

Inside of Me

There's a little boy inside of me,
sweet kid,
shy kid,
scared kid,
hiding from the monsters he grew up with,
talented and clever kid
building walls to protect himself.
Misplaced and forgotten kid,
lost between the very thing he built to survive.
There's a little boy inside of me,
somewhere within these walls.

There is a clown inside of me,
a comedian of sorts,
making jokes,
wearing smiles,
finding humour in the pain,
laughing away the monsters
while whispering words that say
Don't tell people you love them
especially if you love them.
There is a clown inside of me
created and imagined by that little boy
and he likes to turn these walls into a maze.

There's a monster inside of me,
telling me to hate,
saying it's all my fault,
that I am undeserving
I'm useless
unlovable
that there is nothing special about me.
He tortures me,
holds a mirror up to me
and tells me,
You are just like the monsters you've always despised
There's a monster inside of me
because I trapped him inside of me
and he searches for that little boy
who hides behind the clown
inside this ever growing maze.

There is a war inside of me
within this maze of walls
and every day, I hear them speak their words.
Be quiet, whispers the little boy
Hide your feelings, says the clown
Stay silent, yells the monster.
And every day, until today, I listened
without realising all that they say is the same.
But today I'm not a little boy any more.
Today I don't need to make jokes any more.
And today I am not what the monster says I am any more.
For they, like my walls, were built
when I needed them to survive.
but there is more inside of me
than the monster, boy and clown
for there is love inside of me
so much heart inside of me.
And today, I say that nothing will ever be ok
until I can see this world the way I believe it to be.
And as they all finally stayed silent,
I started knocking the walls down.

Her Story

The moment had arrived to engage
with the woman crying on each page,
to prevent her story from dripping,
so not to watch her layers stripping
and tell her these very words spoken
My dearest girl, you are not broken.
In time the sorrowful scars will cease
as beauty's found in every piece.

In these little things we seem to dwell
yet never to speak and not to tell,
but I am here now to catch your tears,
protecting you from all of your fears
and say to you that it isn't wise
to lose all your magic from those eyes,
for I know you're more than versatile
as you create beauty in each smile.

So be yourself, I'll do the mending.
Let's give your book a happy ending.

It Isn't Real

When I cannot fake anything,
I tell myself it isn't real.

> My eyes only weep illusions
> with suggestions of how to feel.

Be happy, it says in my brain
Be broken, it says in my heart.

> For slowly, as I lose my mind,
> my happiness, it will depart.

And I find myself in circles
with imagination gone mad.

> As I am seen smiling away
> with the one thing I never had.

> > Belief in all that is fiction
> > becoming my own autocrat

to lay my body, rest my head
and dream that I imagined that.

> So when I'm awake I don't know
> what this or that is any more

> > and whether it was never real
> > or if I could ever be sure

Be happy, it says in my heart
Be broken, it says in my brain

yet slowly as I lose my mind,
I become happily insane.

As craziness is very real
residing in this complex plot

that I had solely invented
till I became what I was not.

The Friend

My world is fading and I need you

We have all felt this so join the queue

Please tell me that you understand mine

It's okay, everything is fine

Sometimes I feel like this is the end

It'll all work out, for I'm your friend

I have nothing left except my pride

Don't worry because at least you tried

Goodbye and thank you for all you've said

Just keep going, it's all in your head

I am so sorry and I love you…

How I wish that yesterday I knew
and instead had said these words to you:

Dear friend, I truly haven't a clue
of all the things that you have been through
but I have got you and I love you…

Old Soul

She was an old soul in a new era,
feeling out of place with her vintage style,
captivating the contemporary
as a modern girl with an antique smile.

They considered her to be old-fashioned,
seeming out of date and deemed a relic,
pigeonholing this rare commodity
as a woman no less than angelic.

But she was more than just a lost ideal,
meeting this backhanded praise with loathing,
as this lady only wanted respect
and yet was solely judged by her clothing.

For truth be told there was no era
where out of touch was anything but wrong,
yet still she will feel every prejudice
when all she had wanted was to belong.

When You Smiled

When you smiled, I felt like I belonged in this world. In my mind I was the outcast, ostracised and rejected, bullied then neglected and yet when I reflected, your smile left me protected.

Your smile became everything to me, because your smile was the only smile I'd ever felt. My cheeks hurt when I smile and I don't know if that's normal. I often ask myself, did you make me that happy or had I just never truly smiled before and so it hurts every time I imagine when you smiled. When we smiled.

Your lips were like the sunrise and the sunset combined and so everything in between those lips brightened my day. And if you were the sun, I was your moon, waiting for our eclipse, not realising that an eclipse is solely the absence of colour and that after we part, we might never eclipse again.

And so it never happened. It nearly happened. It should've happened, I can imagine it happening and I can still feel your warmth caress me, but it never ever happened.

However, when you smiled, I felt like I belonged as tears ran down my sore cheeks, alone, because you didn't belong in a colourless world. You were destined to belong with the stars and I was destined to be your stargazer. For I will never stop gazing and you will never stop shining and I will never stop loving you and you will never ever stop being the reason that I smiled.

Procrastination

Ripples

You were the rock that skipped across my heart,
turning every ripple into art,
penetrating the surface of my mind
with a dance that was written for the blind.

For I had felt all that I couldn't see
when the ripples began to cover me
before slowly converging into one
as each of your ripples became undone.

And now something inside of me has changed
as your ripples have left me rearranged,
creating a world that I can now view,
as my calm heart begins to skip for you.

Yet I can see no rocks that dance mid-flight
and there are no more ripples left in sight.
Because a rock could never choose to stay –
for you either sink or you skip away.

The Magician of Hearts

The magician of hearts made mine disappear
and replaced it with anger, sadness and fear.

The illusion was never part of her act
it was solely in everything she had lacked

she created her tricks to master the art
believing that this would make love never part

but she didn't expect to feel as mine felt
and she didn't expect to deal as I dealt.

I punished in turn as she saw my heart pound
it beating incessant with deafening sound

then clasped at her chest as she begged it to stop,
insatiably feeding this skip and a hop.

It was true love at work, the ultimate spell:
a magical feeling no one can repel

and it came to the magician at a cost
as she had found her heart the day it was lost.

So she vanished with mine, refusing to yield
as magicians' secrets are never revealed.

Rage

I've struggled too long with this pain
as you now struggle with that chain
your arms wrenched down towards your feet
strapped so tight against the seat.
I see the fear in your eyes
that hold a glimpse of your demise.
Look at what you have done
now the evil has begun
and you're to blame for this commotion
as you made hate my last emotion
festering deep inside my soul
unleashing rage and your downfall.

You had your fun and ruined my life
it's my turn now so with this knife
I look to where I should begin
to slice right through your fragile skin
and with some anticipation
yet without a hesitation
I swing my blade and then my fist,
with all my strength I will persist.
I release my pain. I release my hate
as the beast inside me sees your fate.

And with all my emotions now set free
I stop to admire my artistry:
a missing tooth, a broken jaw
the blood that drips onto the floor
several bruises and abrasions
with umpteen nasty lacerations.
I know your prospects are now bleak,
my lips show joy from cheek to cheek
and as your blood begins to stream
I listen to your final scream.

And never has it sounded so sweet
to hear the music of deceit,
but I know that this will not last
so as you take your final gasp
I get a pen and write this note
then grab my knife to slit my throat
and to conclude without changing tune
I speak as I fall *I'll see you soon.*

To Kill a Monster

To kill a monster is to become the beast
and thus bringing to life what once was deceased.
It is an act that deprives your purity
and yet it is referred to as maturity.

How is it wise to be playing by their rules?
To follow the devil's notebook, made for fools?
It's coursing through your veins like an infection
until you see it in your own reflection.

If we should slay the demons, what of our own?
All that darkness inside which was once unknown.
Should we let live what we have always hated
or kill the evil that we have created?

Empathy > Sympathy

You said at least it wasn't worse, as if to say that my hurt wasn't bad enough. That it had to be worse for you to care.

You said tomorrow is another day, as if to say that I should give up on today before it is even over, because at least I have tomorrow, right?

You said it's not the end of the world, well I can see that. The sun is shining, the birds are singing and the world is turning.

My problem wasn't relative to my powers of observation; my problem was with your abundance of sympathy and your lack of empathy.

And at least my world doesn't revolve around your pity and your lack of compassion, because right now I don't care

whether tomorrow is another day because today is all that I am feeling and today, like every other day, you are not listening

and your empty words are speaking volumes. You are the epitome of why I built a home inside myself, to hide myself from people like you.

The reason why I built walls so high, with a ceiling that I could never quite reach; the reason why the window to my soul has been boarded-up so long.

Yet you stand there, at my door and you tell me that I don't open up but at least you tried.

Well, if you really wanted me to open up, all you had to do was knock. Because I am here. Where the fuck are you?

To the Girl

To the girl who lives in her mind
with eyes wide open, never blind,
a book in hands used as disguise
to hide her story in those eyes.

I do not blame your cautious ways
but shadows only live in days
to masquerade in empty shell
it must be hard to always dwell.

I see a glimpse of beauty there
you hide it well in vacant stare
but you can't stop sparks from shining
or prevent flames intertwining.

And so I write to you in plea
to look at love and set it free.
Don't be afraid to let love shine
for I will catch your sparks in mine.

The Construct of a Thief

I remember a time
when the term forever
was a flawless concept
that I could not sever –
solely an afterthought
as if to break the tide
in waves of emotions
which refused to subside.

However, it was time,
the construct of a thief
that turned my forever
into beauty so brief.
It took my love away
and left me incomplete.
Now lost in translation
I am found in defeat.

Though my clock may not tick
it still beats from my heart,
the unforgiving words
Until death do us part.

Leave Me Breathless

You filled my lungs with air
and taught me to hold my breath,
then took my breath away
and taught me love in my death.
For you left me breathless
when you breathed in our fiction
our beautiful future
and our hopeless addiction.

Yet you breathed out with words
and you spoke with your actions
screaming at our false dreams
to create these reactions,
while I never breathed out
and as you gasped from above,
I fell between your dreams,
to suffocate in your love.

You'd Better Watch Out

There have been many reports of a thief,
with a description that defies belief,
so it is now time that I introduce
you to the very man who's on the loose.
He will get up in your personal space
before disappearing without a trace
and I've heard he's a repeat offender,
swift, although he isn't close to slender.

He judges whether you are bad of good
while terrorising the whole neighbourhood
and even though he has a well-groomed beard
you better watch out as he should be feared.
For if he asks you to sit on his lap
do not get too close because it is a trap.
His hands down stockings, he says it's a gift
as his jolly persona starts to shift.
For the man who's behind that well-made suit
is nothing more than an empowered brute
so be on the lookout, but don't be seen
by the man who goes by Harvey Weinstein.

The Lonely Path

Throughout my life I chose a very lonely path
filled with desolation as I face my own wrath.

And as my pathway slowly floods through emotion,
with each singular tear creating my ocean,
I wonder, would we smile without destinations?
Could we all walk as one without expectations?

And if we cry in unity, our world might learn,
there is a problem here that we all can discern.
So let's break ideals of conformed segregation,
generating pathlessness as celebration.

And if you falter in new-found territory
I'll meet you there so you can stumble into me.

The Gardener's Neighbour

Years ago there lived a neighbour
though this neighbour wasn't mine.
This neighbour was a gardener
or so it said on his sign.
And this I believe, as his lawn
you could never overrate
as this very grass was declared
the greenest green five years straight.

His neighbour always envied this
for no matter how he tried
the grass he grew was not as green
as that on the other side.
He worked hard every single year
yet no amount of labour
could ever make his grass compete
with grass grown by his neighbour.

This angered him so very much
that he chose to make a scene
yelling at the top of his lungs
My grass will be much more green!
To his surprise he heard a laugh.
The gardener showed no fear.
Instead he mocked him by saying
You tell me that every year.

But this year was quite different
as the neighbour had enough;
threatening to destroy his lawn
while his neighbour called his bluff.
When the gardener stepped outside,
it was only then he knew…
as his green, green grass had altered
to a very unique hue.

The neighbour laughed and went inside
but when he came out he saw
a few wild flowers appearing,
then about a dozen more.
The neighbour couldn't stop the spread
as they continued to breed.
His laughter suddenly vanished,
ruined by this nasty weed.

He walked up to the gardener
and yet there was no abuse.
The gardener was truly shocked
when his neighbour called a truce.
He offered him the finest dirt,
however, he wasn't loyal
as it was filled with chemicals
to destroy his healthy soil.

And so this vicious war began
as they plotted and they schemed,
devising many kinds of things
that you could have never dreamed.
Their lawns ripped up and torn to shreds,
gardens rotting in decay
'twas then the neighbours realised
it was competition day.

The neighbour and the gardener
had not anticipated
that both would lose as only they
ever participated.
But the judge ruled that the gardener
would not win six years straight
and neither would his neighbour
as they had no grass to rate.

Infatuation

Your infatuation begins to hold my admiration
but it is your persuasion that is my preoccupation
as all your affection that is headed in my direction
upon my reflection will be the cause of your rejection.

And it's because I envision that your very decision
will be a provision into what will be our division
though I'm no visionary, I'll fall into solitary
when to you what is primary is also temporary.

So please do not misconstrue and try your best not to pursue
as the reason I bid you adieu is because I love you.

The Long Sleep

He was asleep for most of his life,
living his nightmare through,
yet every time he closed his eyes
his heart would dream of you.
And so you began to wake him up
to teach him something more,
and to show him that true happiness
could be worth fighting for.

But how could you ever understand
that the smiles he would keep
would be the ones that last forever
as all he knew was sleep?
For he had dreamed his happy ending
would be when he felt right
and so he swallowed all of his pills
because you held him tight.

For you made him feel so very safe
that now he'll sleep for good
with a smile he thought impossible
and yet misunderstood.
And although your joy survived in him
as a dream never dies,
you took every leftover pill
before closing your eyes.

Your Scar

If I kissed you in one location,
my lips would have traced around your scar,
for your wound may have healed long ago,
but the damage taught me who you are.

If you missed the caress of my kiss,
you would have learnt to be unafraid.
But instead you feared the scar itself,
when it was I who had swung the blade.

If you let me penetrate your skin
and yet dread every single embrace,
it's because your fears have cut deeper,
as misery's easier to face.

Though I cannot promise you no scars,
I vow that my heart's yours to capture.
So lacerate me beautifully,
then kiss me till you're filled with rapture.

If I Hadn't Met You

If I hadn't met you, would I be writing this?
Would I be the same if I didn't reminisce?
Is every word I write, moments we never shared?
Or are they reflections of the one you repaired?
Is that why I'm holding, this pen instead of dreams
when everything is real but nothing's what it seems?
And if I could erase, the memories I knew,
would I be who I am if I hadn't met you?

Green Rose

I was but a sad man, never knowing why
until the day I saw her as I was walking by.
Her beauty in the distance took my breath away
I strolled over to her then asked if I could stay.

She told me in her gentle voice, A challenge I propose;
I will let you stay forever if you find me a green rose.
Her eyes sparkled as she spoke with beauty found within
they shone right through my body and danced around my skin.

I felt my heart begin to race as I accepted her request,
then I kissed her hand softly before setting out on this quest.
I'd never heard of such a thing or whether it was real,
but for her I'd go through this formidable ordeal.

I searched the world until I had the green rose in my hand
and yet this pain inside of me, I could not withstand.
I held the rose and thought of why I still felt so alone
before deciding that this quest I would for now postpone.

Would she even love me? How could I ever be sure?
Am I stuck to live this empty life without a cure?
I had to ask this flower, I needed this to settle
so I asked, *Does she love me?* as I pulled off its first petal.

Yes she does, no not now, as the petals fell
till there were no more petals or an answer to tell
So now I sit here with no rose and with no girl to hold
wondering how I had let all of this unfold…

As it was I who chose the life of the condemned
and in my hand I can see where my problems stemmed,
so I'll bury these remnants then walk away as it grows
for I can pick the girl but I will not pick the rose.

Beauty in the Darkness

Does a tear ever fall out of line
when holding a future memory,
stoically hidden from the author
who created the imagery?

The past had carried every sadness,
so that the present was unrepressed.
For a circle doesn't change its course
when the very inside is depressed.

But now it's consumed by another
placing love between my affliction.
And so this beauty in the darkness
has created its own confliction.

Although I am fearlessly empty
with a numbness, completely unjust.
I know that your eyes could free my heart
if you are the one that I could trust.

And so I'll turn to you and release
all my pain, my weaknesses and fears.
Though my gaze may be underwater
I love you enough to show my tears.

To the Woman

To the woman who reversed into my car and then drove away…
I want to…take you out…on a nice date. I'll bring you white
tulips because red roses are too cliché, too normal and you are
anything but normal my dear. For this night, like you, will be
special. I will drive you to a beautiful restaurant in my newly
dented car. We will sit across from each other so that I can
look into your eyes, moving the flickering candle which sways
to its own ember dance as our fingers intertwined, eyes still
interlocked. You can pick any meal you want as you are my
princess and I want to treat you like no other and show you
how beautiful you are, inside and out.

I'll drive you back to my house, opening the damaged car door
because I'll always hold the door for you. We'll watch a Pixar
movie, I know you're thinking *Toy Story 3* but I believe that the
movie cars, although underrated is the right choice. Like the
moment the king had crashed and Lightning McQueen went
back to help him. While holding your hand, I'll slowly pull
you in for a kiss. My lips will search your body until they have
touched every spot, every blemish because every scratch and dent
is what makes you unique – and you, my love, are imperfectly
perfect and I want you exactly the way you are.

And as the credits roll, I'll hold you tight one last time before
driving you home and walking you to your doorstep.

I want you to be thinking about me as the door closes. I want
you to be excited for our next date. I want this to be everything
that you want. Everything you've dreamed of. As finally, for
denting my car, I will give you the best night of your life and
then not call you back!

Solitude

I heard solitude was peaceful
as all wars are made in numbers
but alas my greatest conflict
is what the recluse encumbers.

With my heavy heart and pale skin
I am the lonely introvert
and so I lock my mind away
to help protect my soul from hurt.

Could this be a depravity?
an immunity to myself
with a cruel lack of compassion
to my soul, my mind and my health,

where I can speak out against wars,
showing that I'm a pacifist
while I smile with pain in my heart,
to contradict this masochist.

Succumbing to the Flame

A gentle breeze fills the room
once covered in thick smoke
helping me to breathe again
and yet instead I choke.

Giving in, I suffocate
playing the victims game
with many ways to escape
I succumb to the flame.

Burnt again, I blame the air
for feeding the fire
telling the wind at my feet
to carry me higher.

Take me into the ember
and please do not return
I have found where I belong
so do not watch me burn.

With oxygen gone zephyr,
this breeze had blown away.
As I fall, the fire dies
leaving me this ashtray.

I fill my lungs one last time
with smoke instead of air
and although I chose this life,
I'll claim it as unfair.

Acceptance

I justify all her tenderness
as a tolerant disposition,
by choosing every consequence
to prove acceptance is her mission.

I whisper my fear while she screams love,
misunderstanding each sudden pause
for how can she grasp this silent heart
of a stranger, till she learns the cause?

So she presses my trigger instead,
to feel what could never be spoken.
Now traumatised by reality,
she endures all that left me broken,

thus casting away all of my doubt,
to believe in this nightmarish dream,
where the moment she became tranquil
was the instant I learnt how to scream.

Beautiful Disaster

No matter how far apart it was for you and I,
we always made sure that we would see the same night sky.
We would look up above, staring into the twilight
believing that together our future was so bright.

But suddenly, one day we had lost sight of our love
and we refused to stop so we could gaze high above.
We started shooting stars, only adding to our woes
and as all the light began to fall, slowly you rose.

I turned to gaze up as we used to; based on an urge,
it was the moment I witnessed a new star emerge.
I watched every sparkle it gave throughout the whole night
with familiar beauty in the shining starlight.

Knowing that it was surely you, I reached for the star
and I could feel that it was true, no matter how far.
So I watched your night glow resting on the water's edge
then leapt toward my love, high atop that rocky ledge.

Until finally in the red sea I start to shine,
becoming yours all over again as you are mine.
And now we feel our light together, sparkling as one
and yet we see others try to do what we had done.

Thus you and I will shine brightly onto that same shore
so this beautiful disaster happens nevermore.

The Smallest Minority

You and I were the little
the smallest minority
believing in a future
without an authority.
We were the sun and the moon
creating our own eclipse
watching as the earth went dark
feeling fear between our lips.
Deep inside, you searched my heart
for something they couldn't keep
but what you found was yourself,
so in solace we would weep.

As from that very moment
we knew the war had begun
targeting both of our hearts
as the moon parted the sun.
Numbers never favoured us
and yet we still chose to fight.
For when does the army's size
determine which side was right?
But you and I were taken
by the world's new-found regime
and with my heart I listened
as I felt your final scream.

They took all they could from us,
claiming our actions treason
when we had done nothing wrong,
with love the only reason.
But they did not understand,
concluding as the end arrives
that if they couldn't take our love
then instead they'll take our lives.
For our light cannot eclipse
this pure darkness in our way,
but our love will still exist
in every yesterday.

Aura

To label one by actions and define them by their crimes
would be the same as if we judged a poet's life by rhymes.
Though written words may whisper as each of our actions speak
the ideology is lost on what we find unique:
from sparkles held in the eyes that create a special vibe
to mystical impressions we're unable to describe.

Whether each anomaly be small or a plethora,
every feeling that we share begins with an aura.

So one may judge from what they see, refusing to reveal
the beauty that they would have witnessed if they dreamed to feel,
categorising what's been done but not what is unknown,
casting guilt on people for certain actions that they've shown
but never who they are or the spirit that is hidden
as beliefs unscientific seem to be forbidden.

However, if one wants to know the truth behind these lies,
they only need to look beneath the sparkle in those eyes.

He Dreams

He knew this was no place for him before he knew what this place was.

By the way that they looked at him.

By the way that they spoke to him.

And by the way they wouldn't speak to him.

He knew this was no place for him when they deemed him too different to fit in, when he didn't want to fit in. He just wanted to be himself.

And he knew this was no place for him when he realised that nobody was listening to reason because nobody ever really truly listens.

He barely speaks now.

He barely weeps now.

He barely sleeps now.

But he dreams.

He dreams that the world will stop judging him by the clothes he wears or the bed he shares or the skin he tears.

He dreams that belonging wasn't based upon similarities but based upon realities.

He dreams that there will come a time where we stop labelling and categorising people for not fitting into our own definition of right and wrong so we can start accepting them for who they are.

He dreams that there is a place for him.

But when he wakes up to a new day filled with every yesterday, he realises that these are just dreams and so he says 'Hi. My name is Andrew and I don't just want to dream any more. I'm exhausted and I'm tired and I know you've all had the same dreams, but dreams are silent and I will not be silenced until this dream comes true.'

Then he weeps.

He finally sleeps.

And tomorrow he speaks until there is a place for him.

He dreams no more.

Remnants

To my tragic supernova,
I promise I'll follow your lead
by letting go of your remnants,
as you attained when you were freed.

I loved every piece of you
that fell apart till your downfall.
So I've picked them up, one by one,
releasing all I could recall.

But if I may just imagine
one last moment internally
it would be of holding you tight
wrapped in my arms, eternally.

Smiling together, one last time,
believing you finally found
the happiness you had searched for,
between stars in the underground.

Would You Please Stay a While?

Teach me who I am,
show me how to curl my lips.
Draw me in your notes
and then write me in your scripts.
Create me a world
where your stories come to life,
then remember me
from this and not through the strife.
Paint me in your mind
as the hero I am not,
then please let me go
So that I can be forgot.

The Invisible War

Thank you all for being here
to celebrate with me,
an occasion where we hear
those special words that we
never allowed to be.

I know we haven't spoken
but I'm grateful you came
for the silence was broken
when you read out my name
then said the war's to blame.

Yeah I was busy fighting
the invisible war
the one that they're not writing
the one that they ignore
the one that I deplore.

But now you all are speaking
of the war in my head
as you're actively seeking
what is already dead
inside a wooden bed.

Thus you all want to riot
ironic chants of peace
the moment I went quiet
yet those words will decrease
and then those words will cease.

For the silence slowly calls
as the world sits in wait,
until the next soldier falls
inside a wooden crate
the next time it's too late.

Second Thoughts

First thing's first, I give out the worst first impressions
and you seconded this motion through bland expressions
because I was not your first choice for a first date,
you saw me as second-rate and not worth the wait.
And yet there you were, giving me a second chance
with the second time around ending in romance.
We reached first base, second base, third base then home run.
You were my first love, first time and second to none.
Till you struck first blood, dishing out the third degree,
having second thoughts as we went from two to three.
I became the third wheel, while feeling second hand,
my second nature second guessing what was planned.
So I thought in third person, doing me no harm,
which helped me realise the third time's not a charm.
As people are more than numbers and a saying;
we can be infinity to the ones staying.

When Beauty Fades

When the world saw perfection in your skin
    my lips were busy tracing every flaw,
touching each freckle that my mind could draw
    to discover the world I was lost in;
for when the beauty fades and wrinkles show
    others won't recognise you any more,
but my lips will find you, just like before,
    and retrace each perfection that I know.

Dominoes

I was born with every piece of me
lined up perfectly
believing that I was free
as I could not foresee
that slowly, out of my control,
this world had taken its toll
destroying everything it stole
as I felt my pieces fall
like dominoes.

Though life had only just begun
my pieces were undone
and even though I tried to run
I was left with only one –
it was my integrity,
not solely an entity
which became my identity,
pushing away serenity.

I searched the entire universe
as I felt my world reverse
and nothing could be more adverse
than a self-inflicted curse.
Until finally in love I found a piece;
finally in life I felt at peace
and I thought that meant the pain would cease
until I felt a familiar release
as the pieces fell, once again, like dominoes.

And so I sit here with thoughts converging
as I feel these pieces merging,
wondering if I'm verging
on a pattern emerging.
For it is all my actions
that now cause these chain reactions
as each piece's subtractions
become more than just distractions.

Because it was what I was taught
this was the disease that I caught
and it was all I had thought
this world ever brought
For me to lay there, once again,
waiting to be picked up, set up
and then knocked down,
falling like dominoes.

No Light to Walk to

This love was real from the first moment,
so don't tell me that this is our last
because I know what forever means
and I refuse to live in the past.

You won't be taken away from me,
I will fight with every single breath
because you know I'd do anything
if it meant I could prevent your death.

If I could, I would destroy the sun
so there would be no light to walk to.
Because if you ever left this world,
all the darkness would spread without you.

I would keep your bright heart close to mine,
then stop time itself for you and I
because I will never let you go
till we both dance in the moonlit sky.

Visions

Take me past your limitations.
Open up your constellations.
Look deep inside my satellites,
and come with me to newfound heights.
Let our diamonds correspond
to see the magic from beyond
allowing us to serenade
ideas of being unafraid.

So leap with me to distant lands
this world we have is in our hands.
With fingers linked let us explore
the beauty of never before.
Our boundaries are perceptions
created by misconceptions
as adventures start in the eyes
and end in our limitless skies.

Mixed Messages

The first time I wrote to her, I was so nervous that I deleted it, only to rewrite the exact same msg over and over again. I must have read those words 20 times before sending it and 20 more after and yet I couldn't tell you exactly what I wrote because the moment that she replied, I forgot. After that, I only read her msgs. I read the stories in her words as well as the stories in her pictures and she told me that she loved how devoted I was to all of her. I began to read her msgs while holding her hand and I would look at her pictures whilst she looked at my eyes and over time, as each day passed, what she once saw as devotion slowly changed in her mind until she began to view it as an obsession. Slowly, her msgs turned into mixed messages and the only time I read her correctly was in the moments when I put my phone down and read her lips against mine instead of her old words, because her new words weren't as kind. But there I was, too busy reading her words and misreading the signs, wondering if she knew that I only checked her msgs when she was there because I missed her even when she was next to me. She's next to someone else now and I'm sure that he can't quote her the way that I can. I know that there is no way that he could remember the position of that sunspot that nobody else notices or the way that her eyes smile or her lips curl. And she, she'll never know that the moment she left, I stopped checking my phone because I missed her too much, and I only got the message when I checked my lips and I couldn't feel her.

Jane Doe

The one of a kind enigma,
unique as he never belonged
found himself a home in her arms
from all of the right that had wronged.

And for a brief moment in time
she promised to never let go
but as her fingers slowly slipped
she became another Jane Doe.

His mystery began to fade
with a rendezvous never planned,
however, they both hoped one day
that the other would understand.

As when the eccentric had her,
all of her love became the norm
with knowledge that each touch she gave
signalled the calm before the storm.

Chalk

My future's past had slowly passed me by
the day that you said your final goodbye,
though I heard the words many times before
in this moment I could sense you were sure.

And all of me felt overwhelmed with grief
as you had become my one true belief,
so believing that we will never talk
is the same as outlining you with chalk.

Because if you have left this life behind
I've already died in your heart and mind;
it kills me inside for life to go on
with the knowledge that you are truly gone.

I tried denial, then shouted your name,
I bargained for hope, with tears and self-blame
but the one thing I could never achieve
is acceptance and thus I always grieve.

So I'll return to the scene of our crime
till your chalk silhouette fades over time,
as how can I admit what you foresaw
when our perfection was the only flaw.

Monster in the Shade

I wonder why hearts race for love

                        yet beat faster when afraid

could this beauty in the darkness

                        be a monster in the shade?

Terrified that all the sun brings

                        is a place it cannot hide

pondering whether its own shadow

                        has something more inside.

Is it scared of its former self

                        or perhaps of future plans?

With knowledge that both night and day

                        is slipping out of its hands,

could this fear be the reason

                        compliments are hard to accept?

While believing every criticism

                        we intercept.

Remembering all that has wronged

                        yet forgetting our own face.

Taking for granted everything

                        that we cannot replace,

thus leaving our lives with empty thrills

                        and sadly no control;

triggering pulsations that will

                        surely lead to our downfall

and refusing to be brave based on fear

                        that we would flatline.

Because many people have the heart

                        and yet they lack the spine.

The Fire's Kiss

The winter's air passed through my lips,
to form a cloud of fog and mist,
till smoke obscured this haze eclipse
of vapoured breaths when the fire kissed.

I felt each ember burn my skin,
and yet there was never a choice.
You knew that I would rush right in,
as soon as I had heard your voice.

I held you as you screamed in pain,
both knowing you couldn't be saved.
Yet I would do it all again,
till my skin's forever engraved.

And when you gave your final breath,
I held you beyond the abyss:
never alone in life or death,
our love was sealed with the fire's kiss.

My Words

Love does not speak, she said, speaking to me,
in conversation, ironically.
And with that, my words meant nothing at all,
tiptoeing off, feeling silently small.

Thus this voice disappeared quite quietly,
as I lacked the words through anxiety.
So instead I witnessed life's frustrations
then reflected on my observations.

And what I saw was just an opinion,
reused by those hoping for a dominion,
who have their own mind yet listen to quotes,
speaking another's without taking notes.

And as these glorified followers walk,
declaring out loud that we shouldn't talk,
using context which is wrong at the core
of an unknown maverick's metaphor,

I simply say, as a reply to her…
nothing…because I quietly prefer
that my words and my love come from the heart,
as they are valuable works of art.

So if I speak to you, please understand
that my love is real and it comes firsthand.

Unfinished

I'm tired of my story. I've heard it each day.
Its colours are fading, ageless yet grey.
It's written with bleakness and yet told in jest
as if to laugh at this life in protest
yet you sit and listen to every word
to every sorrow that had occurred.
You pull me in close, suggesting a coup
to rewrite my history, to start anew.

With my slate now clean, you were my chapter one
but you looked at me different, and with that you were done.
So my story's now changed, you chose to depart…
it was only my yarns that you loved from the start.
And now history has rewritten itself
I place this repetitive book on its shelf.
My story is over, as I chose to depend
and with my lesson learnt, I close my book. The end.

When Fire Met its Match

There once was a time when a rose coloured flame
set fire to a heart which was frozen, yet tame.
He melted with love as she melted in fear
hoping that his spark didn't end with her tear.

She started to run as only water can.
Time was running out the moment they began.
His flame slowly dimmed, flickering without flare.
She knew if she stayed, what little they could share.

But she stayed for love as that would never stop
and ran up to him, until her final drop.
The moment had come, her drop to his ember
and so they combined, a love to remember.

Though tragedy struck, 'twas still a dream come true
as true love prevailed until only steam blew.

Pull the Trigger

I was murdered last night, but slept through the pain,
until your gentle touch awoke me again.

You've appeared in every nightmare and dream,
yet vanish upon a familiar scream.

I feel my throat ache all the way to my heart,
then close my eyes once more, so we can restart.

And if I hadn't known, I'd never figure,
that you would be the one, pulling the trigger.

So I'll close my eyes to reach our final round,
you can kill me, my love, I won't make a sound.

I'll watch the bullet until it passes through,
then open my arms and let this dream come true.

The Lie

This day is solely a pretence
to a lucid illusion gone awry,
a fabricated reality,
with enough truth to believe in the lie.
We are under the influence
of a system that was built to evolve,
leaving our mindsets paralysed,
to believe in a pure lack of resolve.

For we have unknowingly slipped
towards injustice and oppression,
but what's this day without the past,
and our capacity for regression?
So let's disregard what was taught,
for knowledge is power to the founder.
We'll go primitive once again
and then watch the authorities flounder.

What Summer Will Bring

Winter cannot stop me from what summer will bring,
I need to feel the warmth and not just dream of spring.
I'll walk across valleys with fallen autumn leaves,
until I see each pattern that life's highway weaves.

Following the compass that every path creates,
I'll search beyond the horizon for what awaits,
where the shadows are overshadowed by sunlight
that shines upon this golden street all through the night.

till finally I reach the most beautiful view,
for each road I travel will lead me back to you.

Simple

I never was the brightest child, I was what you would call simple. I once saw my dad dressed as Santa Claus and instead of realising the truth, for the next few years I believed Santa Claus WAS my dad.

I used to think that I had an irregular heartbeat because it beat twice as fast as everyone else's, until I realised that ba-bum was only one beat.

I didn't comprehend that racism was real. I once walked past a house filled with people in white costumes from head to toe and I just assumed they were celebrating Halloween early, because it made no sense to me that anyone could believe the colour of one's skin made a person less human.

And I actually believed that euthanasia was about children living in China, because I thought that China was Asia and I didn't understand why the youth in Asia was such a big issue. And while I understand the meaning now, I still don't understand why it's illegal. I don't believe my house is mine, nor my car or my clothes. I certainly don't believe that signing a piece of paper makes another person mine and neither does creating one. The only thing in this world that is mine is me. And we are being told that it isn't our decision when it is the only decision that is ours. When I see people in pain, suffering while hearing others say it's a selfish act, I can't understand why they can't comprehend that it's the one thing we can be selfish about. My body and its flaws and scars are mine. My mind may still not be the brightest, but it's mine. My heart may ache and love too much but each ba-bum is mine. My soul is the definition of passion, hidden inside a walking contradiction but it is mine. And my being exists because I choose it to exist as it is mine and this is as simple as it gets. For I am simple. I am simply me.

My Addiction

I'm addicted to the colours
illuminating from your skin
like a psychedelic canvas
with your essence drawing me in.

You create art in my own mind
to appreciate the value
of a priceless hanging portrait
held on by just a thread to you.

Yet from your abstract undertone
the impression that I've received
is, though you are the drug I crave,
your affections were misconceived.

But still I'll take you as you are
and forever I'll keep you close,
deep inside your kaleidoscope
of colours, till I overdose.

My Honest Poem

I could write you a sweet verse
to say there's no one like you
and although it would be true
it must certainly get worse.

For you take my breath away
in every sense of the word
and though love is truly blurred,
your eyes still brighten the way.

Those eyes of yours captured me
with such an innocent spark,
they left me trapped in the dark
and now you're all I can see.

For the reason why it's worse
is because it is perfect,
it's perfectly imperfect,
in every single sweet verse.

And no matter how I try
to say something is at fault,
I receive the same result,
with no answers as to why.

For I don't know how to feel
because I've never felt this,
I have never been shown bliss
and I'm scared because it's real.

But I know that this is true,
the love, the smiles and the tears,
the joy, the fights and the fears,
and there's nothing I can do.

So I could have compared thee
to that of a summer's day,
but honestly I'll just say
that you mean the world to me.

Lightning Source UK Ltd.
Milton Keynes UK
UKHW021847090223
416682UK00014B/1684